Power Packed Success Formulae snippets of wisdom

Kishore Muralidharan

Copyright © 2017 Kishore Muralidharan

All rights reserved.

ISBN: **9781520747002**

DEDICATION

Dedicated to all the wonderful people, who have made my life meaningful. I thank Junior Chamber International for giving me opportunities that have helped me to understand my potential.

Most of all, my wife Kala and my two angels Sharanya & Sharika.. They have made my world beautiful.

CONTENTS

	Acknowledgments	i
1	God within us	11
2	Success by Choice	14
3	Dream Like a Child	17
4	Emotional Control	21
5	Yesterday's Baggage	23
6	Prioritise to Succeed	26
7	Skill & Will the recipe to Success	28
8	Commitment over a Promise	30
9	Reputation built on Charecter	31
10	Dare to Kill Ideas	33
11	Where is our Tomorrow	35
12	We are our Beliefs	36
13	The Lost Luck	38
14	Identify the Purpose	40
15	How Prepared are You	41

16	Let go the Ego	42
17	Seasons of Life	45
18	Delightful Experiences	47
19	Power Dressing	48
20	Time to Wonder	49
21	Believe in your Intuition	52
22	Be Curious	53
23	Choice of Words	55
24	Consumer vs Contributor	57
25	Moods should be Personal	58
26	The Path We Choose	60
27	Our Image in Public	63
28	Experience Differs	65
29	Being Assertive	67
30	Life on Auto Pilot	68
31	Quick Fix Solutions	71
32	Personality and its Development	73

33	Winning Attitude	74
34	Smile with Million Words	76
35	People Management	78
36	Lessons Around Us	79
37	Easy Learning	81
38	Offense as a Strategy	83
39	Rise to the Occasion	85
40	Evaluate Implications	87
41	Creative Problem Solving	89
42	Strong Roots	90
43	Look for the Source	92
44	Impact on Thinking	93
45	Our Responsibility	95
46	On the Information Highway	96
47	Traits to Succeed	98
48	Customer Focus Culture	101
49	Dream to Deliver	102

50	Sprit and Systems	103
51	The Dwarf Kingdom	104
52	Future and Vision	106
53	Failure or Feedback	107
54	Thoughts need control system	109
54	Live the Moment	110
55	Successful Past	112
56	Let go Attitude	115
57	The Background	118
58	Influence	121
60	Break your Goals	124
61	Champions not Leaders	127
62	Significance	131
63	Don't work Hard	132
64	Expectation and Satisfaction	139
65	Leader's Image	142
66	About the Author	146

KISHORE MURALIDHARAN

A leader is best when people barely know he exists
Lao Tzu 4th century BC, ancient Chinese philosopher

ACKNOWLEDGMENTS

I had been planning to write this book on simple management for the common man; since a very long time ,I wanted to put my 26 years of learning from various business organisations into a book,which would benefit young entrepreneurs and future business leaders. I could never have done this without the support of my friends from the Junior Chamber International. JCI is an international organisation which believes that the earth's great treasure lies in human personality ,JCI has helped millions of young people to sharpen their knowledge and create a positive change in them. I had been sharing "management tips" and "success mantras" on social media for a very long time and all my friends encouraged me to put those lessons & tips into a book for all to read .In this book I have compiled few of the success formulas and tried to create a simple book which could be read in a very casual manner and yet convey management lessons in snippets

I wish to thank Dr.V.N.S Pillai, he has contributed some wonderful ideas which I have incorporated in this work. Dr.Pillai has helped me in re arranging the words of my book into a good reading material, I thank him for this great help in editing my book . Miss Krishna Priya gave life to this book with her illustrations .I acknowledge the support of my well wishers Harish Kumar,Nibu John, Shibu Damodar, Dr,Harish, Rajesh Panicker, Manoj Govind,Dr Vinod B Nair and all my friends from JCI Cochin Trainers Forum.

God within us

Many of us believe God is the goodness living inside us which guides us through difficult paths of life with ease by helping us decide what is good and what is not. Each one of us has adopted many qualities approved by God inside us. If we start looking for God in others, we will see the best of human beings. Some believe work is worship and this is what makes them excel in their profession. The moment we believe that all our karmas/deeds have the touch of God or are for His sake, we will never compromise on their quality, because we cannot cheat our God.

People will go to any extent to please God, they will face any hardship if they know that it is the path to reach Heaven. But some people are easily fooled in the name of God. There are many who make their living by cheating the devout in the name of God; even terrorism is being promoted by some by manipulating innocent people's faith. All this is possible because, people tend to be possessive and fiercely protective of their faith. The same principle applies even to relationships.

When we believe in relationships and have faith in the value of true love we will be more than happy and will find peace within us. If we learn to see God everywhere, the best will follow in everything we do, as faith can move mountains and create wonders. This faith translates as faith in ourselves, confidence in our abilities and the perseverance to see tasks through. A living example of this is Mr.Dasarath Majhi, popularly known as the mountain man of India. This illiterate villager carved a road by cutting a mountain single handed using only a chisel and hammer. He carved a path 110 m long, 9.1 m wide and 7.6 m deep through a hillock. He achieved this feat after 22 years of dedicated work; his effort has shortened the distance between his village and the nearest town by 30 kilometres (Atri and Wazirganj of Gaya district in Bihar, India). Faith wins.

"I can see how it might be possible for a man to look down upon the earth and be an atheist, but I cannot conceive how he could look up into the heavens and say there is no God."

- Abraham Lincoln

Success by Choice

The term 'success' is often misunderstood, its scope is much beyond materialistic life. Success is a feeling of accomplishment, which cannot be judged by one's financial or professional achievements alone. We don't know our success stories, they are often judged by others. Success makes us feel good. A little deed too can give us this wonderful feeling .It can be created once we start appreciating every little progress we make .Success does not always come from great achievements, instead try to enjoy each small step we take in our life's journey. This feeling of satisfaction will make life more meaningful and we will taste success every day. Let's not wait for the 'D Day'.

There is nothing called the D Day, the moment you reach your goal, the satisfaction is short lived and it may remain with you, not even for a week, the struggle of a life time might have given you the fruit of your hard labour, but still the moment of satisfaction for achieving the success is short lived. It is normal human nature to look for another goal and aim for it. Once we keep hopping from one goal to another one success to another, there is no sense of achievement in spite of achieving so much in life.

We tend to forget to celebrate success, we forget to acknowledge our achievement, and we forget to thank all those who walked with us during our tough journey to achieve our goals. The moment we realise the meaning of real success in life, we might have a different definition of goals and a definite purpose for life.

Be at war with your vices, at peace with your neighbors, and let every new year find you a better man.

-BenjaminFranklin

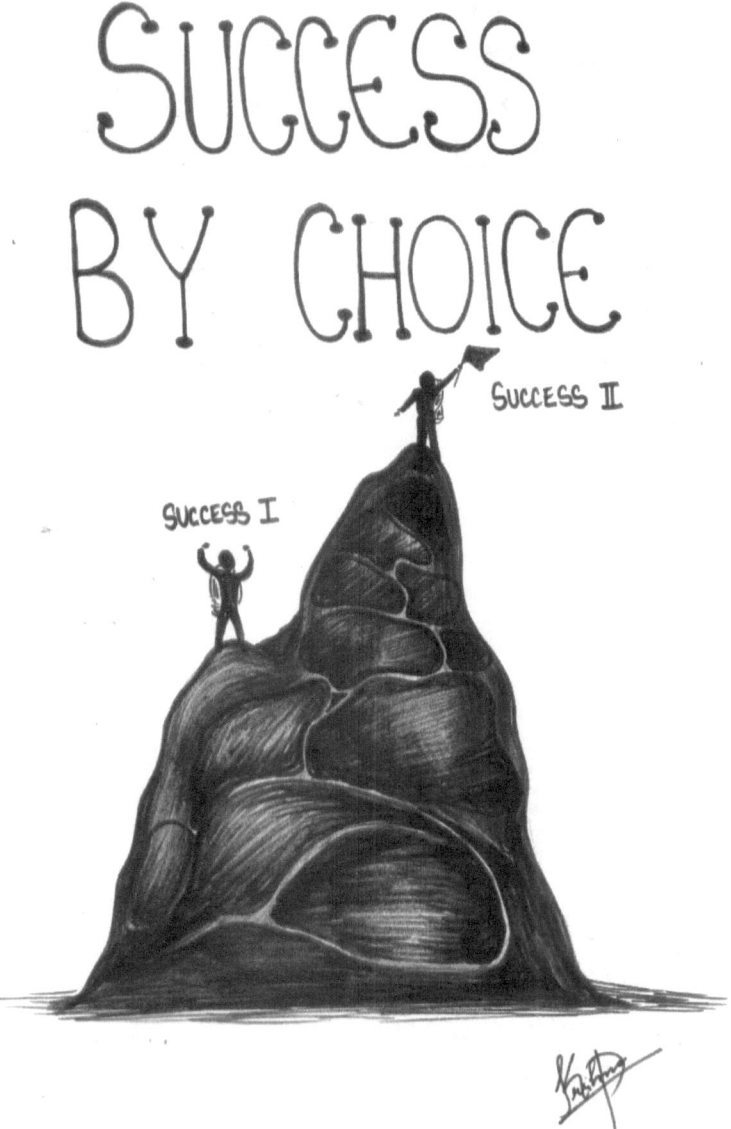

Dream like a child

Dreams with wings can only be seen by very few adults. Some dreams are reserved for the little ones, who have not set any boundaries for their thoughts. The mind of a child is like a clean slate with no prejudices, many wonderful and crazy ideas take birth and grow in such fertile little brains.

Each one of us can have the privilege of dreams with flying cars & chocolate city, but for that we should shed our adult ego and be prepared to get excited at things around us; unfortunately the adult in us finds all these silly. The moment we get out of our glass house of ego, we can enjoy the pure fresh air of life around us, life is beautiful the moment you look at it with an open mind and enjoy its blessings like a little baby, who giggles at every little fun. This is the environment where creativity blooms, relationships flourish and mind is set free to explore with no baggage.

It is difficult to break free from the adult ego-state, we are bound by responsibilities and we believe that we as adults should follow predictable behaviour .Any individual who moves away from this path is considered to be a rebel or some might even think that there is something wrong with the person, who is taking a different path. The power of curiosity is present only with the little ones, it is this curiosity that helps them in understanding the world better. When adults become curious, they create great innovations. Galileo would have never discovered that the sun is stationary, if he was not curious enough to question the belief of their times. We all know how he was punished by the church for this rebel like thinking.

If we remain contented with all that we have, we would not grow. The more curious we are about things around us the faster we will grow .The drive to create a better life would make us move faster and we get motivated when we are dissatisfied with the status quo .Children who gets bored quickly often seeks new toys, the same logic applies to us too. The faster we get into the child mode of thinking, the better challenging and fun filled will be our lives.

Let's enjoy that bliss filled life.

KISHORE MURALIDHARAN

DREAM LIKE A CHILD

EMOTIONAL CONTROL

Human beings are born with emotions, and we were very expressive with our emotions as children. As we grew up we developed control system and higher threshold levels. These not only helps us in controlling emotions but many people are able to manipulate emotions successfully as the situation requires. As we grow up in age, we tend to create a definite image for ourselves and many such images do not allow us to show emotions of weakness. Our emotions are to be controlled in public particularly when we face difficult situations. In such situations our emotions might turn ugly and the scars we create on others during our distress might be too deep to heal.

We can make life beautiful with pleasant and positive emotions of love and happiness.

Though expressing unpleasant emotions may hurt others, there could be situations we need to express our feelings and we should respond to situations. When we respond emotions do take their position and the same will be transmitted. Unless we express our emotions our communication would be incomplete and we might not be able to convey all our thoughts effectively. It is always advisable to express positive emotions with magnification and at the same time we should put a conscious control on our negative emotions. Emotions do have a very powerful impact on the people we interact with. We should be aware of the intensity of our emotions and their implication.

You cannot have a positive life and a negative mind. -Joyce Meyer

Yesterday's baggage

Baggage is the burden we carry along. We often forget that we choose this baggage without even realising. We always had the option of shedding it, but we never think of doing it.

Past experiences give us immense wisdom and we know failures are our best teachers. It doesn't mean that we carry it with us always. Many of us like to treasure our memories, it is a good gesture but these wonderful good memories should give us a lot of wonderful feelings, sense of achievement; some experiences will go with us to our grave. It should be our endeavour to offer good experience to people who interact with us. Once we decide to be a part of other's good experience, our approach and behaviour with others would be very different, as the objective which we have set for ourselves is to make others happy. We will be committed to give them a memorable time in our company.

The troublesome part is when people carry their bad experience in their memories and they influence their day to day activities. People go into depression because they don't let go unpleasant experiences. Failures in life are never to be forgotten, those are unpleasant experiences but they should not haunt us .The lessons what we learn from failures is more important than the failure by itself.

The best thing we can do is, put our baggage of failures & burden in a locker and keep moving ahead with all the vigour and positivity. We can always get back to our quarantine locker and look for relevant lessons from the past when needed. Remember heavy baggage will never let us move ahead in peace or pace.The choice is ours.

We should not give up and we should not allow the problem to defeat us.

-A. P. J. Abdul Kalam

baggage

Prioritise to succeed

Our priorities can make or break us. Most of us find it extremely difficult in prioritising our day to day activities. Many do not even prioritise their short term & long term goals. In the world of multiple options, we need to learn the art of prioritising, or we would be confused with every deed and every need.

Many failures are due to errors caused while understanding situations. We experience undue stress not because of lack of time but because of our wrong priorities. We all have 24 hours each day, yet most of us feel short of time. Successful people master the art of prioritisation, we may be surprised how they are able to stretch their day so well accommodating so much in such a brilliant way, they are able to manage their work, attend numerous meetings, entertain guests, spend value time with their family and friends yet you will find them having spare time for their hobbies. This is no ordinary feat, this requires tremendous amount of planning and practice to lead a life of freedom with commitment and responsibility.

The day we learn the magic of prioritisation, we will know how to make most of our allotted 24 hours. Conscious effort and proper planning are all that is needed to change our lives.

Skill & Will the recipe of success

The success has many recipes but the most important of them all is the attitude. The attitude to put the extra effort, the attitude to remain positive in the most demanding times and the attitude to take people along. There are two elements that moves an individual to success they are skill and will.

Skill is as important as attitude that cannot be overlooked. We have to acquire new skills every time when there is a change in situation, as we know that change is a continuous process. So is the knowledge up-dation.

If we develop an attitude for continuous up-dation and a-never-give-up-approach. Success will come in search of us.

Never stop fighting until you arrive at your destined place - that is, the unique you. Have an aim in life, continuously acquire knowledge, work hard, and have perseverance to realise the great life.

- A. P. J. Abdul Kalam

Commitment over a Promise

Credibility of an individual is built over years, it needs lot of hard work and commitment to be acknowledged as a credible person. One of the main trust building factor is our reputation of honouring promises. The reason why some of us break promises is because we try to please every body and end up making promises which we are not sure of honouring.

A promise is what we assure others, what is more important is our commitment towards our promise. A commitment is the promise we make to ourselves.

A promise may break but a commitment should be solid like rock.

He who cares for his values would never give an empty promise.

However difficult life may seem, there is always something you can do and succeed at.

-Stephen Hawking

Reputation built on Character

Reputation is a certificate bestowed upon us about our credentials, by the people who had interacted with us. People and organizations work very hard to create good and positive reputation. Many even take professional help to create it.
For an individual character determines his value. It is the sum total of a person's personality and

attitude, hence the personality of a person is built on the foundation of his character.

Character is very delicate and it is always in the public domain. Every positive activity of ours keeps adding plus points to our character, but unfortunately negative marks are too high in this subject. A small wrong step is enough to pull us down from the high pedestal and some mistakes can even destroy our image. Let's be very careful about all our actions and build a very strong reputation.

Dare to kill ideas

Everything we see around us were mere ideas once. Our business or career or even profession are all the result of successful idea implementation. What we have today is because of the brilliant idea we had once worked upon.

The fact we all shall keep in mind is that nothing will be relevant for ever, not even the success we enjoy today. The successes were built on yesterday's ideas and need not survive in tomorrow's environment. That is why we should start questioning our own 'successful' status and start working on new ideas for tomorrow.

We shall not fall into a paradigm paralysis with our current situation. We should dare to break free from its shackles and build on new ideas for tomorrow.
Let's remember that tomorrow is not an extension of today.

KISHORE MURALIDHARAN

Where is our tomorrow

We all plan and work hard for a better tomorrow. Often we forget that today is the tomorrow we had dreamt of yesterday. We had worked very hard to create this wonderful today, but unfortunately we fail to recognise this beautiful day and we start aiming at some other tomorrow.

Let's sit a while and think a bit about our today, let's live our today too, because this today of ours has the contribution of many people who worked along with us to create this day for us.

What is the point in planning all our life for an unseen tomorrow which we fail to recognise? We pass by many days we had dreamt of but alas we go blind. Let's cherish yesterday, live our today and work hard for many tomorrows.

Do not dwell in the past, do not dream of the future, concentrate the mind on the present moment.

-Buddha

We are our beliefs

Our belief systems are formed from our experience, exposure and knowledge. The life's lessons we learned over the years influence our thought and behaviour. A person living in Siberia can never believe that life is possible at 54.4 °C in Timbuktu.

We can create beliefs and it can change our outlook. Only convincing exposure can bring in the required change in our belief system. Knowledge from books can be a good source of wisdom, but it is our interpretation of the subject that would influence us.

Let's open our minds to the vast world of experience.

The lost luck

Everybody wants luck to be on their side. Luck is the booster that moves our life to a higher pedestal. Luck may be a mere coincidence that we encounter in our journey called life. To be lucky we should be there where luck is present.

Let's look at this scenario: A person cannot get a job if he does not attend the interview, even if he attend the interview, what if his performance is poor, what is the point in cursing the lady Luck?

Luck is everywhere in the form of opportunities which many of us fail to see. Luck is more about being at the right place at the right time that too well prepared.

"To fall in love with God is the greatest of all romances; to seek him, the greatest adventure; to find him, the greatest human achievement."

-Raphael Simson-

Identify the purpose

The reason why certain people prosper in a particular area is - they could identify their purpose of life and could move in the desired path with full focus. We all can excel in our work or career only if we have a burning desire to achieve the set objective. This current task should be a part of our strong desire.

We work for a purpose, stronger the purpose, stronger will be our desire. This burning desire would give us extraordinary power and passion to work towards our goals.

When we have sharp focus and burning desire, we can feel our goals moving towards us and the impossible tasks would seem achievable. Let's seek the purpose keeping in mind nothing is beyond our reach.

How prepared are you?

Have you ever wondered how prepared you are to meet with a critical life situation? Unexpected call for finance is just one example. In life we may have to encounter situations which we never even thought of in our wildest of dreams.

Turmoil in life can come in many forms like terminal illness, death in family, accidents, loss of job, divorce, natural calamity etc.

We cannot be prepared to face all challenges head on, but we should at least be able to face some with better preparation. Planning for the rainy day approach is one such tool which could help us tide over many situations. Economists term it the 'precautionary motive'.

Good finance management and proper planning would protect us from situations which needs financial strength. Insurance is another tool that can be effectively used as a cushion in unforeseen situations. As the insurance people say 'insurance is a good policy'. The most important support system of all is our strong relationship with family and friends.

Let go the ego

People would never accept mistakes easily. They find many reasons to rationalise and substantiate their faults. It is a very common human behaviour. We think that we can never do anything wrong and we believe that we are the most reasonable persons around.

This is the kind of image we carry about our self. The moment somebody points out our error, we fight tooth and nail to defend our stance and in the bargain we go all out for that, we may even offend the person with a different view. Many wars are fought in the backdrop of boosted ego of a single individual.

It is better to ask our self the cost of letting go, and we would realise that, it only makes us win hearts. It is not touching the headlines that is important but touching the heart lines of people are more important, JRD Tata used to say.

Seasons of life

We all are very familiar with the various seasons and its climatic conditions. Our body reacts differently in different climates and we take all the care to ensure our comfort. We use umbrellas during rains, woollen to fight cold and so on.

We can notice different climates in our life too. These are different conditions and situations we encounter in our personal, professional, family life and career. We face the cycles of ups and downs, plateaus of comforts, steady moments, sharp falls or quick rises. Most of the time we stand perplexed wondering what to do. Its the time for us to realise these life variations and take required protection like we do during each season. Let's be prepared always.

Delightful Experiences

Life becomes lively when it gets filled with delights. We all are aware of customer delight, it is a concept by which many organizations try to get more business. They offer customers something more than what the customers paid for. It has been observed that delight is high when it is offered in the form of experience rather than in kind.

We cherish wonderful childhood memories even after many decades. Discounts and gifts have very short life, where as a warm welcome with a sweet smile and personalised address with first name will go a long way as far as customer loyalty is concerned.

We all love to feel delighted, let's not forget that even the people who interacts with us have similar expectations. Delight comes from recognition!

To enjoy good health, to bring true happiness to one's family, to bring peace to all, one must first discipline and control one's own mind. If a man can control his mind he can find the way to Enlightenment, and all wisdom and virtue will naturally come to him.- Buddha

Power Dressing

What we wear is what we are; is it true? This is the perception many people carry about others. Our dress is our reflection, it could be a perception. Why should we create a neutral or negative impression when we can make the first impression better? Great statesmen focus a lot on power dressing and they put forward their personality without even uttering a single word.

Gandhi ji is the only exception because he was much above all these. He was a saint and a mass leader, Gandhi ji's personality was so strong and his simplicity was his strength. As an ordinary individuals, we can put forward a better self with appropriate dressing for the occasion.

Time to wonder

Life is precious and yet short, this earth is a beautiful place and has so much to offer. We are too busy to enjoy nature's beauty, we seldom notice a flying butterfly or a wandering squirrel, Nature is full of wonders. How many of us have seen a sun-rise or full moon rise or sun set in the last one year? In all probability the answer would be in the negative.

We all know that the lost time will never come back, yet we are least bothered. When we are old we wish we were young enough to do so much, but as young men we never feel the importance of living life to its full. We work too hard and save too much for future. It may sound funny, but we as adults still believe that our childhood days were the best, it's because we had the freedom to fly, fall, jump, climb and run.

One can still enjoy life, just take a look around and feel the little wonders.

The best and most beautiful things in the world cannot be seen or even touched - they must be felt with the heart.

-Helen Keller

Believe in your intuition

Nature has given us the power of intuition, many situations that we encounter might seem familiar, it's because we might have had intuitions about it. Many a time we can accurately judge situations or people from their looks and behaviour, it's because of the experience we had in the past with similar situations or people, We might have forgotten them but somewhere deep in our mind our experience would guide us with signals we call intuitions.

Intuitions are developed from our past experiences which lies in our sub conscious memory. Let's not confuse intuitions with superstitions because superstitions are beliefs thrust upon us by others, it has nothing to do with real experience. Superstitions may be understood as convictions not based rational evidence. But then all beliefs are irrational. If you have evidence for a thing who are you to deny believing it? You have to.

Believe in your intuitions and you could never go wrong.

Be curious

Each moment in life is different and has something to offer us. We would not be able to differentiate one moment from another, unless we observe them carefully. It's our curiosity that makes our observations meaningful and identify the unique features of each moment.

In our career, profession or even in business, we come across many successful ideas but most often these ideas are not easily visible in spite of them being around us for a long time. It is only the person who is aware of his surroundings and situations who can sense these ideas. Let's be inquisitive and be aware of each moment, we might strike gold.

Choice of words

Language is the greatest tool, which binds individuals. People with better skill in handling this tool can go a long way in life. The most influential people are experts in language and communication. We cannot imagine a world without language, a strong leader has to be an expert in communication. Every day we interact with large number of people using various communication media like telephones, electronic mails and also by direct personal contacts. We use different styles in each of these mediums.

The strength of any language lies is in its usage. Right words has the power to move nations, at the same time poor selection of words can cause deep negative impact on relationships. It is worth taking the pain to learn the art of choosing right words in our communication.

Some words are good enough to convey the strongest of message in the simplest of language. When Krishna Menon told his co-passenger Englishman "You have picked up English and I have learnt it" it was a strong message to one who was looking down upon Menon's English.

Consumer vs Contributor

Independence Day is a reminder of the struggle of millions of people of this great nation. We are a young generation who did not have the opportunity to be a part of that great freedom struggle. We have had the privilege to be born in a free nation and just because of that we fail to understand the value of freedom.

We are enjoying the little facilities this country has been providing us. We often compare these facilities with that of other developed nations and find reasons to complain. Let's take an oath today to become a contributor to nation building. Every positive deed we do for the people of this country or for our surroundings or for the government can be our contribution.

Moods should be personal

We come across people who burst out in public causing embarrassment to everybody present there. Moods are creation of our mind, it is the response of our brain to certain external factors or the influence of external stimulation on our thinking. A person with unpredictable mood is always at risk of hurting relationships. Our mood should be too personal and we have no right to spoil the moods of those around us.

We feel it wonderful to be with people of high energy and positive mood. Such people are always liked by everyone. It doesn't mean that people should never feel low. We all have our own ups and downs, highs and lows, but we should ensure that it remains personal with us. Let's develop the art of emotional balance.

The path we choose

Friends, life is full of opportunities and options. Anywhere we go we see opportunities. Anything we plan there are choices available. Our choice speaks about our taste. We can either go with default available option or search for more. We would be surprised with numerous doors opening for us. It's very important that we select the right one.

We must have had several opportunities in the past and we would have chosen this career, profession or life style. In most of the cases our selections were by accident. There are only few people who had the privilege to live the life they chose. We have no control on our past, let's be alert and choose the best for us for future.

Health is the greatest gift, contentment the greatest wealth, faithfulness the best relationship.

-Buddha

Our image in Public

We all like to be treated well by everyone else, we all love to get appreciated. The best way to ensure good treatment from others is to treat others the same way we wish to be treated. When we are in the company of many people, it is observed that everyone behaves well and it's because the public behaviour of individuals are often well-thought and diplomatic.

It is difficult to judge people from their public behaviour. Human beings know the art of manipulation and we can easily feign behaviour if required and we are good at it. Our true public image can be judged from what others speak about us in our absence. It's our real evaluation. We should consciously try to work on our public image. Let's ensure that people speak well about us even in our absence. It needs sincere effort and hard work.

KISHORE MURALIDHARAN

IMAGE IN PUBLIC

Experience differs

As we know, we are guided by our beliefs. These beliefs are embedded within us since ages. Most of these beliefs are our own creation based on our experiences and knowledge. No two individuals will have the same experience in a particular situation, because experience too has influence on our personality.

A cockroach on the dress will be different experience to different individuals, some might scream, for some it is filthy, some may just brush it off, for some it's just an insect and would have no problem even to hold it in their hands. Though the situation was just the same, the experience and response might be totally different to different people. The same is applicable in every situation, only the degree would vary. The best way to respond to a situation is to become aware of it and try to be as logical as possible .That would bring out a matured response to a situation.

Being Assertive

We always like to have a positive and pleasing personalities. We see these qualities mostly in successful people. These qualities are their strength. At times we compromise on our stance to satisfy others and by doing so we might please others but at the cost of our individuality. We avoid giving our opinion, fearing that our view might hurt the sentiments and mood of the group. We wish to satisfy everyone and hence we go with the crowd.

There is no harm in voicing our opinion and by doing so we wouldn't sound aggressive. We are only being assertive. Address issues, not individuals. An assertive statement is a strong statement that is made keeping emotions at bay but at the same time putting across our view or observation. Here the focus should be on the subject and not any individual. We should learn this art of making assertive statement without being offensive.

Life on auto pilot

When we hear the word auto pilot we would immediately connect it with flying. Yes, in flights there is a mode called auto pilot, by activating it the aeroplane flies all by itself following the path pre-defined by the pilot. Have you ever wondered how often we are on autopilot? We would be surprised to note that most of the time we are on auto pilot, because we don't use conscious effort every time, for example we only plan to travel from point A to point B. Once we plan, we automatically start our car, change gears, negotiate through the traffic, listen to music and we reach the destination automatically; while we are on the wheel our thoughts are elsewhere, we are neither aware of the lyrics of the song that is played on the FM radio nor we are aware of the fragrance in car. The moment we become mindful and aware of things around us, life becomes beautiful

Quick fix solutions

We are aware that our world is moving on a fast pace; we find it very difficult to catch up. Speed is seen everywhere and many of us have learned the trick to move with time and at its pace .In this bargain we lost out on many other aspects of life. We have no time to sit and relax nor does our time permit us to spend few moments with childhood friends.

The biggest challenge before us on the fast track is our impatience and irritability, when things go wrong. Our negative behavioural changes will be clearly visible when there is a breakdown in the system. This is the time when we have to calm down and find a solution to the problem .Our impatience pushes us to take shortcuts and quick fix solutions to the situation. These quick fixes would further pull us into its quick sand. Let's not look for easy solutions to big problems. We should give some respect to time and find permanent solutions.

KISHORE MURALIDHARAN

Personality and it's development

Personality development is considered to be the key to success. We often come across people who claims to be experts on personality development, most of them teach only spoken English. Personality is the unique identity of an individual that makes him stand out separately in a group. It is the sum total of his character which includes behaviour, emotional status, skill, knowledge, intellect, social behaviour and so on; there could be a long list.

Our personality is dynamic and our current personality is developed over years and it get influenced with each new experience, because experience and knowledge change behaviour and we know behaviour is a major component of personality. Personality development is done to polish some of our traits and make it visible to the world around us in a positive light. Only experts with psychological skill can do justice to this job. Through proper scientific training this positive change could be brought about. We can concisely bring positive change on our personality if we know where it hurts.

Winning Attitude

Attitude makes or breaks us. The moment we put across a positive posture with a confident look in our eyes, we will see a different world. A world with opportunities, friendly and helpful people. We might also find the system too working in our favour. It is because our surroundings will respond to us the way we want it to respond. It is precisely the principle given in the 'Alchemist'.

A negative person would always find the going tough, they would only see problems where ever they go, even the people they meet are trouble makers. If we observe successful people, they seldom use the word 'problem'. In fact it is better to replace problems with challenges. Problems are roadblocks whereas challenges have solutions hidden in them. Let's move ahead with positive winning attitude and we will see many success stories on our way.

Smile with million words

We all know that our face is the mirror of our mind and all that we want to say can be expressed using non-verbal language. This medium alone in isolation cannot express us fully. Our language can be controlled and we could use verbal or written language to express many things which we might not be sincere about. Verbal or written expressions cannot be full unless our body language emits all the signals to convey the real meaning of each word we utter.

We all wish we had the magic wand to create good relationship with people and the best way to build relationship is to make the other person comfortable in our company. The toughest of situation can be handled with a genuine smile. It is the most powerful and positive gesture of all. Let's spread smile it's like fragrance and its effect is contagious. A genuine smile is worth million words. I recall here a pharmaceutical company's gift to me with the slogan engraved on it "Smile! You are better now!"

People management

Managing people is an art we have learned in the most natural way since childhood. As children we knew how to influence our parents and get cakes and toffee. Little babies know how to attract attention of others with their sweet giggles. When we grew up we became very conscious of our behaviour and our natural response is lost.

Today we interact with many people and have to depend on each other in a social setup. Successful manager is the one who gets his work done by others, that too without causing any discomfort to the doer. There are a few people whom we should appreciate for their man management skills. It is because others eagerly wait for an opportunity to work for them. This is the kind of relationship they have developed, they have done it with love and care. We don't manage people, truly we manage ourselves according to the situation and other's expectations.

``

You must be the change you wish to see in the world.

-Mahatma Gandhi

Lessons around us

We may have friends who are voracious readers, hooked to self-help-books. These people will be never seen without a book in their hand. We would be surprised by the miracles these books can play on individuals, if they follow the lessons learned from those books. The sad part is some people never change in spite of reading hundreds of such books. Reading is a great habit, what is more important is absorbing relevant contents from these books and implementing those in our lives.

It doesn't matter the number of books you read, even a single book is enough to transform us. We see trainers quoting numerous authors and their books, but unfortunately they are unable to connect with real life experience. We should observe around us, there are great lessons to learn from life. As a trainer one should be able to connect one's life experience to the training content. This would increase one's credibility as a trainer.

Easy learning

We grew up playing with lots of friends as children, those were the days we did so much together. We had opportunity to do so many crazy and adventurous activities. The fun of togetherness was our motivation to do those interesting yet funny and at times embarrassing crazy things. When we look back we would find those days as the most memorable ones and friends of those days would always remain our buddies ever after many decades. It is because when we do challenging activities together as buddy team, the bond between us gets stronger and a long lasting relationship is developed.

This is exactly what is expected of an effective Out-Bound-Training (OBT). In a well- crafted OBT the relationship among the team members should get stronger and they develop into a very committed & effective team. This not only happens within the organisation but would go beyond working hours. In OBT the kids in us are brought out into open to play and learn together.

Offense as a strategy

Offending someone is always considered an aggressive and negative behaviour. Anybody using offensive action is considered to be a threat to others. Many intentionally use offense as a strategy, the best place to evaluate such strategies are the battle field or the corporate world. In both these places offensive as well as defensive strategies are used to win over the enemy or the competition.

We might use offense as a strategy when there is a threat from our opponent, we could use this to weaken our competitors before striking into their domain area. Offense is the best defence, they say. We can become offensive when we feel that our defensive mechanism is not strong enough to withstand the strategy of our competitor. Here we go all out with unpredictable assault and capture the market or the territory when it was least expected. Great wars are not won by strong army but by wise strategy.

You will not be punished for your anger, you will be punished by your anger.

-Buddha

Rise to the occasion

When the sailing is smooth, there is nothing much to be done, because the calm sea will take us safe. It is during storm that our skills will be put to test. In crisis we get opportunity to rise above the rest and prove our leadership. Challenging situations are the testing field of the real mettle within us and our ability to manage situations. Critical situations would panic us and some of us may even give up and escape from a deteriorating situation, it is normal human behaviour of escaping from troubled waters.

Escapism is not what we expect from a leader. We all know that the easiest way is to avoid a situation and not get involved. Any Tom, Dick and Harry can do it. At the time of crisis the real leader would emerge and he would take initiative and rise to the occasion and manage the situation successfully. Our real testing time is at the time of crises and challenges when all our knowledge and skills will be put to test. Let's ask ourselves are we ready to lead?

Once you replace negative thoughts with positive ones, you'll start having positive results. Willie Nelson

POWER PACKED SUCCESS FORMULAE

Evaluate Implications

We know the Newton's third law of motion in physics, which says every action has an equal and opposite reaction. This is not only true in science but even in real life this law is very much true. The only difference is that the reaction might not be of equal and opposite. The implication of our actions could be very different.

In physics we can quantify each action with a reaction but in human behaviour this could be very different. The intensity of reaction could vary with people and situations. Successful people are good at understanding the implications of their actions, they do it even before they act. If we consciously try to understand response to our actions, we would be more careful about them, and this would help us in dealing with people better. Every experience enriches man. So his reaction to two similar situations will be different. His experience in the first situation enable him to take a different stand in the second situation though situations are similar. Let's create positive relationships with our action.

Creative problem solving

There is no situation in life without problems, we should not shy away from problems. It would only make the issues bigger. We know the saying 'a stitch in time saves nine'; the same holds true in problem solving, the more we avoid unpleasant situations, the bigger they become. When issues grow to mega size, it would not be easy for us to manage it alone.

Challenges are part of our recipe called life. We all know that we should face problems or challenges head on. There could be easier ways to solve problems if we start looking for unconventional methods. Once we understand the core of it, solutions can be found in various forms.

All that is needed is identification of the root cause and look for out of box solutions. Traditional solutions may not be easy always.

Strong roots

A tree grows strong and tall when its roots go deep and spread wide to get the required nutrition for its growth. We need our own strong roots to help us grow, our roots are our connections, knowledge, intelligence and our emotional balance. All the connection and contacts, which we develop from our childhood days contributed to our growth by providing us the nutrition of relationship.

Knowledge and intelligence helps us to identify the right and wrong, they also help us to take the right path. We have been acquiring knowledge since our birth and this is a continuous process, the moment we stop learning we are as good as dead. Emotional balance is developed from our relationship. The art of building relationship is not easy, understanding other human beings is very tough. Our emotions are the building blocks of our real self. Let's stretch our roots far and wide and reach for the best nutrients for our wholesome growth.

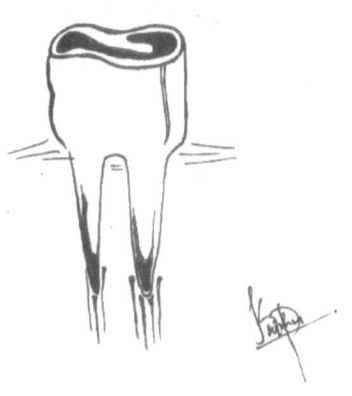

Look for the source

Many challenges come to us every day. This can happen in professional and personal life. When we face challenges, we immediately pull up our socks and address it, without much delay and try to get over the situation. We do this because we know that if we delay action, problems would multiply.

Ever wondered what the real challenge is? We seldom think of the root cause of the problem. Many of us look at the periphery only and the visible issues. If we probe deeper, the root cause may be something totally different; unless we address the root cause, we would be only treating the symptoms.

Power is of two kinds. One is obtained by the fear of punishment and the other by acts of love. Power based on love is a thousand times more effective and permanent then the one derived from fear of punishment.

-Mahatma Gandhi

Impact on thinking

The journey of life is long, filled with experiences. Some of them may be very encouraging and a few may even discourage and disappoint us. In a life time we witness and participate in innumerable events. Each of these experiences contribute to our knowledge and maturity.

Many a time we fail to recognise those life changing events, we even forget them after few days. Our conscious mind might forget events but these might make a permanent mark in our subconscious and would influence us in our behaviour and response pattern. Situations and events are inevitable, they keep happening. It's our awareness that can protect us from negative influence of events.

To succeed in your mission, you must have single-minded devotion to your goal.

-A. P. J. Abdul Kalam

Our responsibility

This world is unique and complete. Nature has provided us everything that man wants. This place is a gift of God, we all come here as guests and utilise all the facilities provided by nature and return.

The sad part is we never behave like a guest on this earth. We all start believing that we own this planet and start abusing all its resources. Each one of us has contributed to the deteriorating condition of the natural resources. We pollute air, water and land without a second thought. We should understand our responsibility towards our surroundings. We know that there is everything on this planet to meet our needs, but our greed would not be accepted by the nature.

We are quick to blame the system, the government and everyone else for all the problems, we have this knack of shying away from taking ownership and responsibility. Our awareness and concern for environment will make us a responsible guest of this Planet.

Optimism is the faith that leads to achievement. Nothing can be done without hope and confidence. -Helen Keller

On the information highway

Today we are once again in the ICE age. Information, Communication and Entertainment have fused together and is moving at the speed of light. We might find it too difficult to keep pace with this. All the three were present since time immemorial, it is only the medium and pace that have changed. In olden days information was passed from one generation to another through verbal communication, and were there was a possibility of distortion and filtering in the process.

Development of script has revolutionised communication .The pace was slow but such communication had very long life. Our religious books are the best examples of this. Today with the emergence of internet and mobile technology the information sharing is the fastest. We can reach the whole world within seconds.

The life of these information is too short, and we find that these become irrelevant within few days. We often use and quote shared information with others without even cross checking the authenticity or relevance. Let's remember that when we share an information, we are authenticating it. It's our credibility we are putting on stake.

Traits to succeed

There are three different traits observed in successful people, they are Elephant trait, the Horse trait and the Deer trait.

People with Elephant trait follow the principle, "slow and steady wins the race". They move with strong determination, they push through all problems with all their might and wouldn't stop till their objectives are achieved. They may be slow but they are sure to reach their goal. Tata group is a good example of Elephant trait.

Horse represent aggression, speed and force. Such people are too fast, they travel faster than the world around them, they can imagine things which can take shape in future and they are future ready. Their strength and weakness is their speed. They might fall or collapse when obstacles come their way. Two examples I can think of are Patanjali and Sahara group.

The deer is the most versatile animal of the jungle, they can hop, jump, skip and run without any problem. They have the skill to avoid obstacles, they will jump over them or dodge away from them. Some people follow this strategy for their growth. They run a lean mean organisation and they carry very little baggage. They are also big risk takers and have high energy levels. Examples: Warren Buffett & WhatsApp(sold to FB). Let's decide what trait we should adapt for our growth strategy.

Customer focused culture

Today's Success Mantra is focused on one of the most important ingredient of any business that is the customer.

Customers should be the purpose of any business's existence. Successful business models are developed based on clear customer oriented strategy. Customers are the most important asset of any organisation. Customer focus should be a top down approach. The top management should drive the entire organisation through the path of customer focus. Employees follow the path set by their management, it is equally important that there should be a proper synchronization of employee values and organisational culture. Any mismatch would create chaos in the system.

Every employee should be brought on board with regard to organisational policy. A good induction program with regular orientation programs would be needed to create a strong organisational culture. Trust your team, they are the pillars of any organisation. Keep open communication with your team, because they are the driving force of the organization, they represent the face of the organisation. We should regularly talk to our people and appreciate them for their commitment and customer focus.

Dream to Deliver

Dreams are powerful, they can create wonders. Every great thing we see around us started off as a dream, those dreams had attained their logical conclusion. All of us dream of many wonderful things, great projects or mega ideas. It is easy to dream as long as we are not committed to create them into reality. We know that making dreams come true is a herculean task and only very few people have the guts to work on them. The more intense the dream, better is the chance of it turning into reality.

Greatest of ideas are meaningless unless efforts are made to make them into a working model. All great creations started with a spark of idea, which was pursued with a lot of passion, hard work and commitment. Dreams gets transformed to ideas, ideas when pursued with passion and committed hard work, turns into reality. Let's dare to dream big and "do" to deliver great output.

Spirit and Systems

Some organisations are vibrant and they are always on the move. They are on the fast track of growth and are bitten by the creative bug. There are two factors that lead to organisational vibrancy. These organisations are built by people who dare to question norms and they are passionate about what they do. It is their Spirit that keeps them moving ahead of competition.

Growth cannot come through organisational spirit alone. Spirit should be supported by proper systems in place. These systems guide organisations in following path of success. Lack of systems could make successful ideas to fall flat. Successful formulas are created by spirited people with mad passion working in an environment of uncompromising organisational systems. Spirit and systems together can create billion dollar organisations.

The dwarf kingdom

No one is indispensable, nature has its own way of replacing people. A good manager is one who is aware of this natural phenomenon and he creates a successful replacement for him. Some people live in fools' paradise and they do not want to make way for others. They cling on to their position and they would go to any extend to hold on to their position for rest of their life. They use politics and ego games to remain in their current position. These are the people who find no place for them in future. They realise that they are incapable for taking up higher responsibility.

When people reach to their maximum growth potential, they realise, that if they help others grow they might not find a role for themselves in future. This is the reason why they feel so insecure and prevent growth of others. They tactically move out all potential people and build a team of dwarfs around them. These dwarfs are also an insecure bunch with no growth potential. Thus a tiny kingdom of dwarfs is formed with an iron curtain. Their path only leads to slow death of the organization. One should be vigilant of the development of such whirlpools and move out at the earliest before the bug of incompetency bites.

Future and Vision

Today world is very dynamic, there is no longer a rare event but daily phenomenon. We are no longer surprised by change. Gone are the days when people resisted change, today all understand that change is inevitable and most of us have transformed ourselves as change agents. The mobile technology played a great role in our behavioural change. The apps in our mobile phones have taught us to move fast with change, we feel outdated if we don't change our phone every 6 to 12 months. We go crazy with virtual Pokémon hunt.

The fastest growing organizations are built on strongest technology, and they are driven by people with great vision. Older generation always resisted change, I'm no longer surprised when I get face-book and other social media friend requests from my octogenarian uncles and aunts. They once kept computers at bay, today they feel uneasy when their wi-fi goes off. This is the greatest proof of acceptance of change. We knew that if we fail to adapt to changing trends we are pushed to obsolescence. Let's look ahead and embrace change as future belongs to those who move faster than change, with greater vision.

Failure or Feedback

Failure disappoints us the most, because we fail to accept the true outcome of the event. We are unhappy with failure because the results were different from our expectation. What is expectation? It is nothing but a page from our wish list. Many factors influence outcome from an event, we as common men prefer to have predictable outcome. We get very upset with unexpected results. Sometimes people get happy with negative outcome, it is because they had anticipated negative result.

We are not trained to face failure. We get very upset when our calculations go wrong. Some people go into depression and some end up with suicide, when failure stares at them. Let's understand that failure is just an outcome of an event, which means, it is a feedback from the incident. Once we start accepting failure as feedback, we feel more comfortable and we would not feel like a looser. Feedbacks are essential to correct our mistakes, feedbacks are there to help us improve. Recall the case of Edison who lost two million dollars on a project; he said by spending that he understood that it will not work.

Thoughts need control system

Our thoughts are generated in our brain, it is our response to external stimuli. Some of these simulations might have happened long ago but its impact would remain with us and it might exhibit itself at various situations. Some of these responses might embarrass us and we would agree that such responses were totally uncalled for. Our responses need to be responsible. It is our awareness that matters, once we are aware of our thought and its impact on our behaviour we would be better equipped to manage our response.

Some thoughts are very strange and their impact on our response system would be equally strange and strong .These are the thoughts that we need to become aware of, we should consciously bring in a control system to prevent involuntary illogical response to situations. Mindfulness and awareness could help us bring in control to our thoughts and response.

Live the moment

Life is a mystery. Everyone is curious to know about the unknown side of it. We are happier to live in the imaginative future, which is gloomy and difficult. We tried to be prepared to set the unknown tomorrow. It is very unfortunate that tomorrow of our imagination is very dull, frightful and often a bad day. Our mind likes to help us prepare for the worst and precisely for this reason it shows a negative, gloomy and very difficult future. This causes worry to many and we jump to our bad future through our imagination and we start living there. If we happened to ask anyone the reason for their worry they have numerous convincing reasons to give. Spiritual leaders and yoga gurus advise us to live in the present. But our mind would only show us the future or an unpleasant past. In the bargain we refuse to see the wonderful today; the bad tomorrow we had anticipated yesterday. When we meet with reality, we know that today is not as bad as we had imagined, we don't try to learn our lesson about our pessimistic mind, rather shift our focus to the future; the future with over a million challenges.

Our mind has a special ability to shunt us back and forth like a loco engine at a railway shunting yard. Our journey backward is the ride to the past and we spent some time there, enjoying the good experiences that we have had or we crib about the problems we had encountered there in the past. Our selective mind picks up all the bad experiences we have had since our childhood days; it is willing to show us a never ending tragedy film or a horror show. Our mind is like a film director with a great creative imagination of future. It is like a gypsy story teller who loves to tell us our own stories; with incidents which has no relevance to our present, or which might have painful experiences which we always wanted to forget.

Successful Past

How often do we think about our successful past and cherish those moments? How often do we re-live our beautiful past experiences through imagination? Our mind has the ability to recreate wonderful moments anytime we want, but we are not ready. We always like to feel sorry about ourselves and our selective unfortunate experiences. It reminds me of an incident which Sri Sri Ravi Shankar, the 'Art-of-Living' Guru had once mentioned in one of his sermons, he mentioned about a business leader who wanted to de-stress his life.; this corporate head was always under stress, he was stressed about his future, stressed with the past non-performance, tired of his company and stressed with his manager's performance. He was gloomy and tense always; his only request to Sri Sri was to help him get rid of stress from of his life.

The advice given by Sri Sri was "live in the present and keep a smile fixed on lips" every time; his interactions with friends subordinates and colleagues improved. This simple prescription worked for the man and his life changed for good. Living in the present moment is very difficult because of the mind's swinging nature, the only solution what we can have is count on our blessings; whenever our mind swings backwards - to our past, we should guide it to some of our wonderful experience with an enjoyable incident . This would stabilize the thoughts and stress can be reduced. Enjoyable experience of our past can be used as an anchor to remove stressful and unpleasant experience.

Imagine you had a very rough argument with a customer of yours, and you knew that you have done no mistake, that incident would surely leave a scar in your relationship and moreover you would never be able to meet the customer again with the same in enthusiasm again which you had before. It is because you had few positive experiences which you had shared with a customer but one argument has nullified all the previous positive experiences .This is the reason why you can never be the same person again with that customer.This is a log jam situation where in emotions overall logic. logically you knew that the customer is important to you and you had a good business relationship with him. This relationship would improve your business . An ego class has every potential to undo years of good work ,and what you see is how emotions overrule logic. logic says that your business relationship is a Win-Win for both of you . The unwanted heated argument was enough to hurt both your ego and damage the long association in the past ,both you and your customer might have had hundreds of Pleasant meeting and discussions

;such interactions instrumental in creating a bond between both of you. Years of working together could be negate with one incident of that bad judgement .

Let go attitude

how to bring back the good old days of trust and relationship? This is a challenge most of the people face when they realise that they had rubbed

people in the wrong way. In fact realisation alone is enough to bring in a new approach. Most of the time this realisation does not happen due to the ego factor .It would prevent people from let go attitude. Every time they think of the other person the bad experience pops up and it irritates the mind .This very thought further builds pressure within and hate increases.This then becomes a vicious cycle.

In every human relationship such unpleasant incidents do occur , and most of the people learn to live with these unplesant thoughts .It is in fact stressful for many when they meet their opponent, the mind gets into a negative mood and it would start re -living the unpleasant incidents all over again .Once the mind switch to negative mode, It will reflect in all our behaviour and our body language too would emit negative signals to the other person .Once our language ,mind and body work in tandem in expressing negativity it would never create a positive outcome from our interaction. There are solutions to overcome this negative behaviour ,it is possible to convert our negative thoughts into a positive behaviour .The best way forward is to replace the thought itself. We must have had many happy incidents with most of the people we have had interacted. One silly and unpleasant event must have created at deep scar which over ruled all the previous good experiences we had enjoyed once ;we should realise this tricky behaviour of our mind. We should be able to bring out those good experiences and ponder about this moment ; and all our ill feelings would reduce ,this may even disappear . Every positive experience is a blessing and our realisation about these blessings would help us wash away our feeling of hate and bring out the positive aspects of Human Relationship.

It is very common to find that the worst enemies where once best friends. Similarly siblings who grew up together might become arch rival in business or in profession and they may become bloodthirsty of the other.The reason for this enimity might be very simple;which might have hurt the ego of any one of them this is very much visible in family run business, politics, corporate board etc.. the rivals of today have had many wonderful years of togetherness in their past , the moment they are willing to keep their ego at bay, they would realise how foolish they were in expressing their behaviour in public; about the other individual, let go the ego and you will find a much more pleasurable world full of loving in human beings.

Open your eyes to the forgotten times of good experience you have had and life will be more pleasurable.

The background

Every big tree was once a sapling, every great company started from zero. All great men and women where once a child. Values, systems, processes developed over the years get embedded into their behaviour and it becomes their way of life, this happens even with us-our behaviour patterns have the footprints from our past knowledge, experiences and environmental impacts. A person born and brought up in a desert will know the value of every drop of water, and he would appreciate the value of the water as a precious resource. He would never waste water. Similarly a person who had worked in the army would know the value of discipline, because his discipline alone must have saved his life in the war field.

It is absolutely important to understand the background of our employees, our competition or even our friends. Once we know their past experiences, past behaviour or even their exposure, we would have a clue of the logic behind their response and reactions. Knowledge about the background would not only enable us to understand them better but also we can know their strength and weaknesses .Skills can be trained but the knowledge about the background would help us to identify the right attitude of each individual. Once we can match skill with attitude then it becomes easy to groom them, for example a person born to a farmer must have had a lot of exposure to plants and nature as a kid, and he would have learned the art of gardening and farming in the most natural way, as the part of his growing up process, such individual would be very successful in industry related to farm products or biotechnology and anything related to nature. This knowledge and exposure would make his work passionate.

This is exactly what we observe as the difference

between the alumni of big business schools and ordinary colleges or universities. It is visible that all the products from Top Universities and top business schools get placement offers from good corporates as soon as they are out of their college, whereas students from ordinary institutes struggle to find a decent job .Have you wondered why such a big differentiation happens with respect to students. Both students studied the same course and both hold similar academic qualifications. The reason is simple, it is a exposure to the right kind of people, the peers and the faculty with whom they interact during their academic development .This is true in all stages of growth and development.

Influence

The Company we keep influence in our development and growth. Such elements have great role to play in our overall growth. They play a vital role in the whole development in behaviour and thinking. This difference we see in an MBA graduate. MBA can be studied at various institutes life Harvard, Stanford, Oxford and in India ,Indian Institutes of Management, premier Universities, Government colleges , Government Universities, and even through correspondence .Syllabus maybe similar but the quality of students would be totally different in spite of all efforts put by the student to give himself best of knowledge, student from small time college can never be compared with student of premier institutions of international levels. This is because of the influence of environment of peer learning. The quality of the peer and the faculty would determine the quality of learning, here the learning is not about subjects but it goes beyond textbooks.

Many a student must have missed the opportunity to study in premiere institutions but still there are opportunities available to polish oneself, and they need not worry about the lost opportunity. In fact life is always ready to give us many opportunities. We only need to look for them.

The best thing they could do is to join groups of individuals who are successful, and associate with them, such association would add value to their outlook, and there would be a positive change in their personality. Listening to Ted Talks, lectures and talks of great people are available on the internet, it is an opportunity one should not miss .these would influence in one's growth, there are also organisations and management association in every town, identify them and be a part of the winners.

Correction need not always happen at the grass root level, proper management during growing years too can bring in positive changes in people. All that's needed is the will to give a good try, and take in the best available option.

Break your Goals

Everyone works towards achieving many objectives in life. That is, for every activity we do there is an objective which we aim to achieve. These are called goals. Goal setting is done by many, some with knowledge & acquired skill and some without even understanding the concept. For a layman it is called plan, but most of the people prepare this plan without even knowing the processes. .Some fail and some succeed, they call it their luck or destiny.

Even housewives have goals when they put the milk on the stove, her goal is achieved when the milk boils. She has the goal to put her children on the school bus on time, she has many such goals, and thus her day is full of fixed goals. People from all walks of life work towards set goals these goals could be micro goals, mini goals, very short term goals, short term goals, medium goals, long term goals, very long term goals and ultimately life goals. Each of these goals are interlinked and many micro goals together form a mini goal , many such mini goals leads t short term goals and so on. The ultimate life goal is a combinations of billions of micro goals. One cannot let go any micro goal unattended as we don't know which of these would have an impact on one's life goal. The real challenge lies in identifying those crucial micro goals. Let's look at building a rocket, which is supposed to deliver a satellite 950 km above the earth. Think it as a life goal.

Millions of tiny parts are involved in rocket building. Let's imagine each of these tiny part as a micro goal. Many small parts form a component (mini goal). Many small components together form a machine part, these parts are used to form motors, engines, electrical circuits, coolers, boosters, panels , heaters etc., all these parts put together form the rocket and satellite (long time goals).

The tiny bolts for the rocket are made in special lathe machine and imagine the worker overlooked the setting and a small error of 0.001mm occurred. The bolt produced here would not hold tight under strong friction. When these bolts are used in strapping motors on to the rocket it goes unnoticed. At 225 km above the earth the motor slips as bolts give away due to friction. The entire life goal is missed due to a small error in the micro goal (bolt)and the rocket falls apart and the mission aborted thus a micro goal missed can lead to the entire project's collapse . In the real life the challenge is in identifying such a vital micro goal, which has a direct impact on the medium and long term goals.

If the same bolt were to be used on the satellite solar panel, the life goal of the rocket and the satellite would have achieved since the solar panels do not undergo such friction and the mission would have become a success. We need to identify these critical micro & mini goals and re-set them as per requirement.

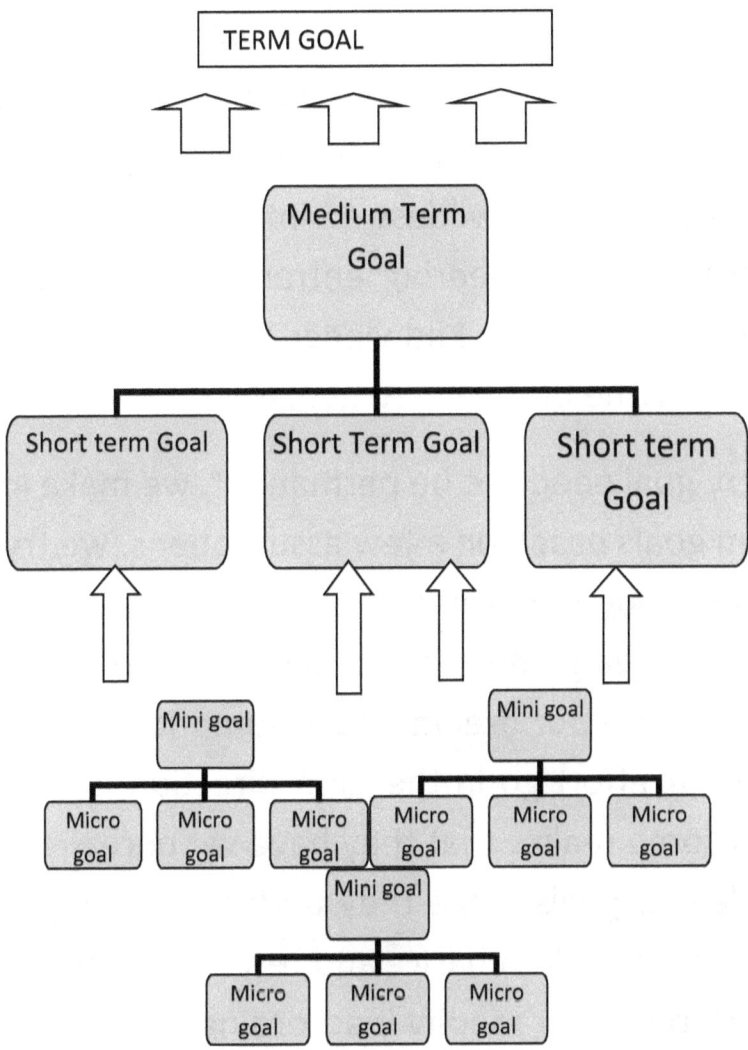

A small boy of 7 years wants to become an engineer like his uncle, for a 7 year old learning multiplication table, odd numbers, even numbers etc. is a medium term goal which he has to complete in a year but the same would form part of his long term goal of an engineering degree. Can you in your wildest of imagination think of passing the engineering entrance exam without the fundamental knowledge of multiplication tables? (One of the micro goals)

Every goal need not be permanent, we make long term goals based on a few assumptions, we try to predict our requirement and objectives for the next 10 years and set our long term goals, most of the time our dream and assumptions are true and our effort go in the right direction, but midway some realize that they have set unrealistic or irrelevant goals, once they understand this, they should go back to basics and rework on their goal chart, redo it or modify it accordingly.

We should be emotional & passionate about our goals but one should never be stubborn with goals. Once we get locked to our goals we refuse to look at other better alternatives and we become blind with our beliefs. One should always look for signals that might indicate the need to modify goals. Let no goal be stone carved, let it be flexible. The new re-set goal should always be better than its earlier version.

Champions not leaders

Most of us have seen how Leadership is bestowed on individuals who have performed exceptionally well in their profession. Professional mastery does not guarantee a successful leadership. Leadership qualities are to be developed consciously and the same is a continuous process. Expertise will certainly help in creating credibility to the leader among his team mates. It would also help the individual in gaining initial acceptance with his team. The journey forward can be successful only if the leader can create the atmosphere of mutual trust, sharing responsibility and team commitment. When Leadership is entrusted to individuals with no people-management ability or administrative skill, they would be a disaster to the organisation, in the bargain the organisation will not only loose a champion performer but at the same time, a great performing team might lose its position due to unforeseen chaos and loss of focus.

People management is a very difficult task and the same need to be handled with a lot of care. The Leadership ability of one person can create wonderful results even from a team consisting of average performers. The enthusiasm and drive from the top can make sea change in the team's performance. The leader's thoughts and beliefs would be transferred to each member of the team and the same would reflect in the result. It is like a virus and it would spread like a wild fire. We can observe that even a new member of the team with very minimal or no direct exposure to leader would show signs of leadership- influence. This is because of the sheer aura of the leader's personality.

It's not only organisations, but even nations turnaround with the emergence of some leaders.

We have seen a small country, became a global financial influencer within a span of 50 years. Singapore was a poor country when it got its independence. It was a country of fishermen whose sole source of livelihood was from fishing. Today Singapore is the economic hub and trading capital of the south Asia. How did this transformation happen in less than 50 years? One man, Lee Kuan yew made this miracle happen. He had a clear vision for Singapore's development. By the 1990, the country had become one of the world's most prosperous nations, with a highly developed free market economy, strong international trading links, and the highest per capita gross domestic product in Asia outside Japan. He made this possible with his clear focused mission. We have other examples of leaders who were given similar responsibilities, Cuba had Fidel Castro, North Korea had Kim Il Sung. We know the difference each Leadership had made to these countries and its people.

Significance

Priorities are set based on importance or significance of a matter. Significance is a very dynamic in nature. There are many factors that influence the significance. Time as influencer: Time decides the relevance of many things. If we are in a hurry to catch a flight we might postpone some activities which might otherwise be important. For example we might possibly postpone a meeting or even a shopping plan if we are late for the flight. It is because the significance of the catching the flight is more important at that point of time. The significance of the flight will reduce if we know that a client is visiting us with a million dollar business. In such a situation we would prefer to miss the flight rather than missing the Business-order. Here we weigh the benefits before we prioritise. Once we identify, what we gain and what we lose, in a particular situation it becomes easy to select our priority. If we have options it is natural that we would choose what is best for us at that point of time. The significance will change dramatically with time. What is the significance of a two day old news-paper? Launch day of a most awaited product holds a lot of significance to its fan. This is the reason why we see long queues at Apple stores during launch of each model of the iPhone. We don't see such queues now, because the significance of the launch is lost after that particular day.

Individual's preference: The first ticket of world cup football finals will be a prized possession for the fan. We might not understand its significance. What is important to one individual need not be of any significance to another person. We have crazy fans during football matches they go to any extend to cheer their team, we have seen fans on rampage after nail biting matches. Those fan give great significance to each match. Antique collectors give great value to their priced possessions. This proves that how significant these materials are for some people. Whereas for others it might be very normal stuff. It is very difficult to give a value rating for everything. We cannot always commercially compare one thing with another, as its value changes with individual's preference and the value what they perceive for it. For a thirsty man the value of water is priceless. Sometimes it is the urgency of the need that determines the value and significance. Low availability and more of demand also helps in creating significance to a commodity, this is pure economics. Understanding this would help us in prioritising our needs based on its significance.

Don't work hard

We all like to be known as a hard working persons, we respect hard workers. The truth is hard working people cannot achieve much, they may succeed in their area of work where in, they would have attained perfection in their skill. Their exposure would remain limited to their area of work alone. If we are to employ someone we would only prefer hard working persons, because we know they would put in extra effort to get things done and would be willing to take up more work without any complaint. Hard workers are workaholic and they seek pleasure in working more than anything else. Employers crave to have such workers on their payroll. To succeed in life hard work alone might not work, because to succeed we need more exposure and flexibility, to attain exposure one should be able to stretch beyond his domain. Hard working person seldom gets time to look beyond his work. They follow a set pattern of work and their main aim is to bring in perfection and to improve their own productivity, their sole focus would be to work more and attain more.

The secret ingredient of successful work is smartness. One should evolve as a smart worker from a hard worker. The smart worker is creative and he finds out ways and means to get his work done more efficiently rather than mere quantity increase. In smart work the focus is not only the productivity but development of efficiency in the system. A smart worker might put less of physical labour but he would design models which would work for him and help him achieve his objective with lesser personal effort. A good leader is a smart worker, he utilises his leadership skill to get his work done by others, more over they do it with passion. There is a saying "never do a work which can be got done by others" this does not mean that the leader should sit idle, he should utilise the saved time to take up challenging job which he alone could handle. He might also take up new role or responsibility for himself .The leader should continue developing others to replace him so that he can move on with newer assignments. This should be the way leaders work, and thus they create an efficient team.

Expectation and satisfaction

Satisfaction is the feeling of accomplishment when we reach our goal. Often we fail to define our goal and because of this we do not know what we have achieved. In such a scenario our joy is limited and there would be confusion if we have achieved what we have had planned.

Satisfaction, very much depends on our expectation. If we are to attend a Rock-Band and expect symphony like performance, we would be a lot more depressed persons, often this is what happens with relationship too. We expect a well-defined or predictable behaviour from the people we meet, but the relationship will collapse even before it takes shape because we had a different expectation from that individual. Our mind had created an image about people even before we meet them. This pseudo-image is what creates opinion about people, most of the time it would be a wrong judgement.

There is nothing called an ideal situation, every situation is unique and hence different, and it is only our approach to the situation that gives it the definite colour. It is human nature to become judgemental about individual or situation, it is because we start looking at them from our own perspective. Our past experience, knowledge and exposure gives us wisdom and ability to analyse and understand people or events. What we fail to realise, is that our knowledge is limited and our vision is not 360 degrees. We often fail to explore the other side of the story. The result of such observation is frustrating as we were expecting a situation displaying only our view and our imagination with a narrow vision. The wide angle view was missing. We should try to understand the full situation from all angles and accept things as they present themselves without trying our glasses of scrutiny, the moment we learn this art, the entire world and all its people would look very beautiful .

Leader's Image

The world's most notorious dictator Hitler and the greatest saint Mahatma Gandhi had their own understanding of the world and they behaved accordingly. Hitler had hatred and violence in his path, whereas Mahatma Gandhi chose the path of peace and non-violence. Both had a clear vision about their ways and both were passionate about them; there were followers for both but the World will remember both these leaders differently. As leaders we too create images about us in our journey called life. We should decide what kind of image we should leave behind. Whatever may be the path we take, it should be unique and there should be messages in it for our next generation or for those who wish to take the path we have shown. We have the choice as to what we want to leave behind. There will be takers for everything, but wisdom should be our guide.

Some leaders are not born leaders nor did they

work for leadership, for them leadership is bestowed upon them by situation. Greatness is thrust upon them, to quote Shakespeare. This is usually seen in family run business or in political families where, the death of the family head leaves a sudden vacuum and the absence of second line leaders brings in a crisis like situation. When Mrs Indira Gandhi, the then Prime Minister of India was assassinated on 31st October 1984, the Congress party had no second line leader since it was a Political family that run the party, it had to rely on Rajeev Gandhi who was her son and a pilot. Mr.Gandhi reluctantly took charge as the Prime Minister of the world's largest democracy on that very day. Those are the real challenging situations, which creates opportunity for the elevation of the unexpected and the unprepared. Persons with no previous experience or exposure are given responsibility many times their capability, only very few leaders survive such a Tsunami, often the trusted lieutenants of the older times have the secret ingredients to successfully guide and lead the organisation or the Party. Proper management of these assets would help the new leader thrive. In the case of Rajeev Gandhi, he not only thrived but was a very successful leader and he is still considered as visionary leader who had brought in technological initiative to India. He was the man who was instrumental in making India the software leader of the world. Leadership is about utilising all the available resources in the best possible manner for the common benefit of the goal achievement.

> *One who enacts obligatory prescribed actions without expectation of the result of actions he is truly a renunciate and a follower of the science of uniting the individual consciousness with the Ultimate consciousness; not one without prescribed duties, nor one who merely renounces bodily activities.*
> *-Mahabharata-*

ABOUT THE AUTHOR

A passionate Trainer with hands on sales management experience of over 27 years in a wide range of industries.

- Post Graduate in Management & with a Degree in Law graduate over 27 years of experience in Training, Sales & Marketing Operations in India and abroad.
- Junior Chamber International certified trainer.
- Authored two books "Leadership Mantras for Success" and "Power packed Success Formulae".
- Fluency in 7 different Languages : English, Hindi, Malayalam, Tamil, Telugu, Oriya & Bengali.
- Presently Managing Director of Fiesta Rubber & Latex Technologies Pvt Ltd ,
- Representing Crusader Chemical co Inc, Baltimore USA, in India ,the world leader in Dewebbers & Deformer chemicals
- A Corporate trainer on Modern Strategic Selling Skills , Business Leadership & Business Soft Skills .

- Involved in developing the world's first Latex ERP, an ERP software exclusive for Glove Industry.
Experience in the sales & marketing of a wide range of products – Pharmaceuticals, Software Solutions, Latex Toys, Latex additive chemicals etc.
- Exposure in Pharmaceuticals selling ,FMCG marketing ,Industrial Selling, International Business.
- Trained over 20,000 young ladies and women from more than 50 institutions on self defence under Project Shield of JCI Cochin.

www.ingramcontent.com/pod-product-compliance
Lightning Source LLC
Chambersburg PA
CBHW020916180526
45163CB00007B/2759